Endorsements for *Land Media Interviews Without a Publicist*

"Penelope Kaye has performed a great service to writers everywhere with her new book *Land Media Interviews Without a Publicist* I found it useful in promoting my own books and will surely be recommending it in the writer's workshops I teach. If you want your book to reach readers, here's a must-have resource."

Nick Harrison
Author of *Magnificent Prayer*,
One-Minute Prayers When You Need a Miracle,
and *Power in the Promises:*
Praying God's Word to Change Your Life

"Penelope Kaye's book *Land Media Interviews Without a Publicist* is the most understandable book on how to secure a media interview. She describes what it takes for a writer to be prepared and knowledgeable for this type of marketing. Each key helps build the author's skill, confidence, and professionalism to present his/her book for a distinct audience."

"Penelope makes you feel as if you are sitting across the table from her while she gives clear and specific guidelines. She takes the fear out while revealing the necessary components. Because the eight keys are easy to apply, anyone can adapt them for their own books. Her approach is heartwarming and encouraging. Every author needs to pick this up as a resource."

Janet Feil
Author of *Day by Day:*
Thriving After Sexual Abuse and Trauma

"Thank you, Penelope Kaye, for not just giving us the keys we need to land interviews but for clearly showing us how to use them to unlock doors. I highly recommend this helpful resource."

Marlene Bagnull
Write His Answer Ministries

"In her book *Land Media Interviews Without a Publicist* author Penelope Kaye shares Insider Secrets to help you become a guest on media programs around the country. Self-published authors especially can tap into Penelope's grass roots system (created out of necessity), a process that's resulted in Penelope being a guest on dozens of programs…so far."

"From the step-by-step research guidance, an explanation of broadcasting lingo, and suggestions about making the call, Penelope covers it all. If you've longed to step into the world of media interviews but wondered how, wonder no more. Buy this book today."

Patricia Durgin
Online Marketing Expert, Writer, Speaker, and Host of Marketers On A Mission, the FB Live program for Christian writers and speakers

"I am pleased and delighted that Penelope asked me to endorse *Land Media Interviews Without a Publicist*. As a radio host, I have received many long, boring, unsolicited press releases that cause my eyes to glaze over. Reading this book blesses me in knowing that Penelope turns a dull transactional encounter into a relationship through research.

"Radio is 24 hours a day, and you, as an author, should feel as though you help fill that time with valuable information our listeners will appreciate, making our jobs easier. We do not want dead air, something Penelope emphasizes. Take it to heart and be energetic and eager to help us fill our airwaves!

"Her well-researched keys will pay off, if followed and made your own. She has almost convinced me through *Land Media Interviews Without a Publicist* to write a book just so I can promote it through radio stations all over!

Jack Canfield, author of *Chicken Soup for the Soul*, said, 'Writing a book and not promoting it is like having a baby and leaving it on a doorstep!' Be a 'situational extrovert,' apply Penelope's keys, and go for it!"

Jackie Mahr
CRMC (Certified Radio Marketing Consultant)
Host of "Share His Light Ministries",
KCRO Radio, Omaha, NE

Land Media Interviews Without a Publicist

LAND MEDIA INTERVIEWS
•
WITHOUT A PUBLICIST

8 ESSENTIAL KEYS FOR AUTHORS

PENELOPE KAYE

Land Media Interviews Without a Publicist
Copyright © 2021 by Penelope Kaye

All rights reserved.

No part of this book may be reproduced in any form or by any means—whether electronic, digital, mechanical, or otherwise—without permission in writing from the publisher, except by a reviewer, who may quote brief passages in a review.

The views and opinions expressed in this book are those of the author and do not necessarily reflect the official policy or position of Illumify Media Global.

Published by
Illumify Media Global
www.IllumifyMedia.com
Let's bring your book to life!

Paperback ISBN: 978-1-947360-87-7
eBook ISBN: 978-1-947360-86-0
Library of Congress Control Number: 2021911981

Typeset by
Tammy Goodman

Cover design by
Robert Sauber
Tammy Goodman

Illustrations by
Haley M. Hoffner

Illustrations copyright © 2021 by Haley M. Hoffner
All rights reserved.

Printed in the United States of America

About the Author

A teacher who loves to write, Penelope Kaye has managed to combine both throughout her life. Whether penning profound poetry, children's picture books, or adult non-fiction, she pursues excellence in her craft. Her teaching career spans decades, including public school, children's church, adult education programs, and homeschool. She also teaches writing courses for the local adult community education center.

The author of two books, *Making Crooked Places Straight* and *Land Media Interviews Without a Publicist*, she has written columns for area newspapers and is a highly respected annual reviewer for the High Plains BookFest. Her devotional, "In the Dark and Loving It" won "Best Devotional" for the Oregon Writers Cascade Awards.

While her two adult daughters live on opposite coasts, Penelope Kaye resides in Montana. She enjoys walking, doing word puzzles, and eating blueberries anytime of the day. You can find out more about Penelope and her various projects by visiting her website, PS2710.com.

Contents

Foreword		X
Introduction		XV
Key #1	First Things First	1
Key #2	Website Wrangling	6
Key #3	Which Words?	16
Key #4	Other Media	22
Key #5	The Call	32
Key #6	Media Kits	48
Key #7	Follow-up	74
Key #8	The Interview	
Author's Note		83
Acknowledgments		85
Appendix A		86
Appendix B		93

Foreword

"I don't know if I'm doing enough to promote my book. Can you help me?"

I was speaking at a writers conference in Estes Park, Colorado a year ago, when a first-time author pulled me aside to solicit my feedback.

"What are you doing right now to promote it?" I asked.

"My publisher didn't give me many tools to promote my book, so I decided to start with radio stations. I found a database that lists every Christian radio station in America. Eventually, I figured out what to say, and now radio producers think I'm a professional publicist."

"Wow!" I replied. "How many radio stations have you been on?"

"Oh, I don't know. Around twenty with another twenty to go."

"Wow! That's amazing!!"

"Really?" she replied rather sheepishly.

"Penelope," I explained, "you've been more successful in promoting your book than most, if not all, of my authors."

That was my introduction to Penelope Kaye.

Two months later, I asked Penelope to join me for our monthly authors' training. They needed to be more like her. I also urged her to write this book to share her discoveries with you. Hiring a publicist is expensive. An Illumify Media author hired one for *only* $4,000 per month—with a three-month minimum. That's what you can expect to pay.

But what if you could learn to become your own publicist? With a little hard work and perseverance, you can save thousands of dollars and open many of the same doors as an expensive publicist.

Here's what I love about Penelope's book:

Penelope proves that anyone can do it. Seriously, anyone. No formula exists to give you the secret to selling lots of books. If it did, every publisher would follow it and make boatloads of money. BUT, if you've published a well-written book and you follow her example, you WILL sell more books.

From the moment I met her, I was amazed by Penelope's inquisitiveness. She researched, learned, and refused to be defeated by whatever challenges stood in front of her. Perseverance isn't a gift; it's an attitude that any author can acquire.

She's not a famous author (yet) nor does she have a publisher willing to shell out thousands of dollars to promote her. She's a normal person, just like you and me. But she did it!

Penelope pulls back the curtain of how radio stations work. If you've never worked in the radio industry, the whole production seems shrouded in mystery. I mean, you don't even know what the radio program host looks like! But she gives the basics of how they work and think, and which stations you should and shouldn't contact.

Penelope gives you clear instructions about who to contact and what to say. A teacher by trade, she presents easy-to-understand templates and shortcuts that will help you. In Key #3 she lays out a glossary of the various terms and definitions you need to know to appear "legitimate." In Key #5 she tells you what to say. And if you're interested in other media, she gives you the basics for that arena in Key #4. Follow her instructions and you *will* generate interviews. Really!

Penelope gives you assignments to build those PR muscles. Feel overwhelmed at the prospect of hunting down radio stations and contacting station managers? Don't be. Penelope gives you small chunks at a time to master. As you exercise those PR muscles, you'll get more adventurous and, ultimately, sell more books.

Since the Great Recession of 2008, every author has borne the primary responsibility of promoting their books. Even bestselling authors. The "barriers" to get on the radio (high expense and lack of know-how) prevent most authors from even trying. With the keys Penelope gives you, the barriers don't seem so formidable and your promotion will set you apart from other releases.

For such a short book, it's jam-packed with helpful information!

Michael J. Klassen
President and Publisher
Illumify Media Global
IllumifyMedia.com

Introduction

Congratulations! You wrote a book, signed a contract, and have a release date. It's time to sit back, let the publisher market your best-seller, and enjoy the royalties!

Uh, no. Unfortunately, in today's publishing world, much of the marketing falls to the author. And truth be told, most authors don't like to, don't want to, and don't know how to actually market their books.

Thankfully, writers have numerous resources to help, including online courses, workshops, and conferences. *Land Media Interviews Without a Publicist* gives you one more tool to put in your arsenal to let people know you and your book exist.

Hello, I'm Penelope Kaye, an author just like you. And . . . I didn't like any aspect of marketing my book; not to mention, I didn't have a clue how to go about it.

However, I found out. My education into the marketing arena came primarily from attending writers conferences. At my very first one, I signed up for a continuing session on the topic. Even though I didn't have a manuscript ready to submit, I knew I needed that class. I learned a great deal; however, before the end of the first hour, I discovered more of what I didn't know.

After some years, I eventually pitched my manuscript to an editor; the publishing house offered me a contract; and I came face-to-face with the beast called marketing. In spite of all my efforts to learn and understand the business, I realized I still had a huge learning curve.

Pondering the marketing material from a variety of sources, I decided to pursue radio interviews. I took a leap of faith and made my first call. In the beginning, I didn't know what to say or who to talk to. Still, I kept at it, and now program directors think I'm a professional publicist.

Before we dive into the actual keys, I want to highlight a few items. Concerning the writing style, I wrote it as a tutorial for authors without publicists. It's a straightforward how-to book with eight keys, giving specific instructions, lots of examples, and helpful assignments. Please keep this in mind while reading it.

Regarding the assignments, each one is designed for the specific content just covered. However, at some point, you may find it easier to combine the two tasks from Key #1, First Things First, and Key #2, Website Wrangling. Also, at the end of each chapter is a NOTES page for you to jot down thoughts, reminders, or key points.

While this book's major focus covers radio, I included a section to discuss different media outlets for interview opportunities. I chose this approach of a number of reasons, which I detail in Key #4, Other Media. Not only will you will gain the necessary information you need to make informed decisions, you can adapt any of the other material in the book to fit the specific direction you choose in your pursuit of interviews.

When writing about program directors and producers, I debated which pronoun to use. I tried to do the he/

she form or switch back and forth, but it became too cumbersome. I settled on using "he" simply because the majority of the ones I spoke with were men. Why more male than female? That answer, my dear friend, is for another book.

What you're about to read in the next pages will give you the necessary tools to land interviews. I'll share what I learned about who to talk to, what to say, how to find stations, and much more. While I can't make any guarantees, by putting these skills to work, along with perseverance, you too can fill your calendar with a variety of interviews across the country.

Let's get started!
PENELOPE KAYE

Key #1
First Things First

As I shared in the introduction, my first endeavors to obtain radio interviews began in a rather clueless state. Didn't know who to talk to. Didn't know what to say. Didn't know where to look. However, my ignorance did not deter me. Google came to my rescue, and the rest is, well, not quite history.

To give you the edge I didn't have, the first key, finding radio opportunities, along with other media, still begins with Google. Since I wrote a faith-based book, I Googled "Christian radio stations." A number of sites came up. After clicking on several to see what they offered, I finally settled on https://www.christianradio.com. It listed every Christian station by state and included FCC (Federal Communications Commission) data, which provided more detailed information. I started with Alabama and proceeded to write down the call letters for every station in every state, along with any other information I thought would help.

Googling the call letters came next. I learned to recognize which stations had a streaming format rather than individual programming. This bit of insight narrowed my list and saved countless hours of unnecessary phone calls. From there, I went to each station's website. Every single one. Obviously, I spent hours and hours looking at them. However, without investing the necessary time early, I would have wasted a lot more time later.

Ready for your first assignment? Get a notebook, legal pad, or spreadsheet. Go to Google and search for the type of station you want to pursue for your interviews, i.e., classical, sports, country, public broadcasting, Christian, contemporary, etc. If you do want Christian stations, then use the website listed above and add "/stations" when typing the address into the toolbar. You will go directly to the page with a dropdown for the stations without having to sift through all the information on the home page. Also, under the FCC information, if the location is Rocklin, California, delete it. These are K-Love stations, and, as of now, K-Love does not interview authors.

Next, decide how to organize your list. Then, assuming your data begins alphabetically, start with Alabama and write down the call letters and any other pertinent information. Leave enough room for follow-up notes if you plan to make calls from your list. I did not, and eventually ran into trouble trying to decipher what I wrote while trying to conserve space. Necessity led me to develop a spreadsheet to keep all the information organized. A free template of what I used is available from my website, www.PS2710.com. See Appendix B for the download code.

NOTES

KEY #2
Website Wrangling

By now, you have a long list of station call letters. A really long list! While overwhelming, the next action will streamline those you need to contact. The second key covers several facets of website wrangling.

For radio, a strategic aspect involves recognizing which ones provide streaming services only. In other words, if a station's entire programming comes via satellite or the internet, the owners/managers will not have the capability to offer author interviews. Unfortunately, many of them already use this format. However, don't despair! Plenty still want to provide their listeners with interviews from authors.

To start the process of elimination, open your browser and type in the first set of call letters followed by the word "radio." While appearing obvious, occasionally, other businesses will use the same letters. Adding "radio" removes confusion and saves time. Hopefully, you will see call letters followed by ".com, .net, .org," etc. These stations, for the most part, do not stream their programming and will potentially have the ability to do interviews.

Any of the following domain names above the call letters signify streaming/satellite services:

- tunein.com
- radio-locator.com
- radiolineup.com
- mytuner-radio.com
- streema.com
- radiostationnet.com
- ontheradio.net

Delete these stations from your list. Their programming is already set in a continuous loop with other speakers and/or music. While those listed above cover the majority of streaming options, you may run into a few

Focus on the call letters with their own domain names. They offer the greatest opportunities for interviews. While the potential for paid programming or streaming still exists, these stations have staff, equipment, and a building or office.

Let's use WZZA Radio, a station in Alabama, as our example. Type the call letters and the word "radio." You will see WZZA Radio with its own domain name—www.wzzaradio.com. To the right will be a description of the station from Wikipedia. You can either click on the domain name or check out Wikipedia. I usually glance at Wikipedia's page first because it provides helpful information to know before I access the website. For instance, you might find out the station no longer exists or airs under a new license/name or has a sister station. Those tidbits can be beneficial in the search for interviews.

Now comes the wrangling. Navigating websites can be as simple as prancing in the promenade at the beginning of a rodeo or as challenging as roping a pesky calf hoofing it across the arena. By using the time-honored Five W's and How, prancing should win over hoofing.

Who

Getting to the right person in your first call saves time. Look for the tab entitled "Staff." Does someone have the title of program director or producer? If yes, write down his direct email and/or phone number. If not, can you tell who handles the programming? Smaller stations don't always have the luxury of these paid positions, so you may need to talk to the owner or general manager.

What

Find out the type of programming the station airs—religious, sports, country, music, talk, classical, etc. Some will have a "Programming" or "On the Air" tab. Several stations have a "History" tab so you can learn their roots as well as their focus today. The information you discover is critical to determine if the theme/purpose/message of your book will be a good fit for the station.

In addition, you may be able to tell if the programming is already pre-recorded or if some shows have the capacity for interviews, live or pre-recorded. Other stations list the entire programming schedule, allowing you to see which ones are produced locally versus nationally. As an observation, local programs offer a better chance at snagging the interview.

When

Note the hours of operation and time zone on your spreadsheet. Make calls during their operational hours, not necessarily when it's convenient for you. You will have a greater likelihood of talking to a real person, rather than a machine, when you place your call. Also, try to determine which program has the best fit for your book. Jot down the host, title of the show, and the time it airs. If you mention it in your call, the program director knows you've done your research.

Where

Check the "Contact" or "Connect" tab for addresses and phone numbers. Some stations are affiliates for larger corporate media companies. You may need to talk to a person in a different state for programming information.

Why

Before including a station in your list of prospective calls, you need to ask yourself why. Why this station? What have you discovered that keeps certain call letters on your list? Better yet, have you listened to any of the programming? Time is valuable, especially in the radio industry. As a matter of fact, time equals money. It's a precious commodity to you and the program director, so don't squander it.

Once you choose to approach a station, make sure you know the answer to the "why." Not only will your pitch flow when you hear "Hello" on the other end, you will appear professional and worth listening to, valuable traits when asking for an interview.

How

The "How" aspect of website wrangling deserves its own key. We'll go through the process of asking for an interview in another chapter.

As we come to a close, now would be the time to make sure your own website presents a polished look. A poorly done one poses a stumbling block. Many times the program directors pulled up mine while we discussed my book. Because it came across as inviting and professional, they saw me, the author, in the same light.

For your second assignment, we'll double dip. Eliminating stations while determining which ones present the best option appears rather daunting, particularly when seeing hundreds of them. Consequently, bite-sized pieces win the prize. Start small. Set a goal of getting through one page a day. Or work on one state at a time. You don't have to wait to make your calls until you've completed the entire list. Once you have a reasonable number, pick up your phone. I made my first ones after finishing all the states starting with the letter "A."

In the process of streamlining your list, take time to review your website. You want it to present you and your book in the best possible way. If you don't have one, check out those of your favorite authors. Pay attention to what you like and don't like. Talk to other writers and ask their advice. Perhaps your publisher can help you. Use the internet for resources and support. Some companies provide free templates. If you prefer and have the finances, invest in a professional designer. Either way, make every effort to have your site up and running by the time you make your first call. You won't be sorry.

NOTES

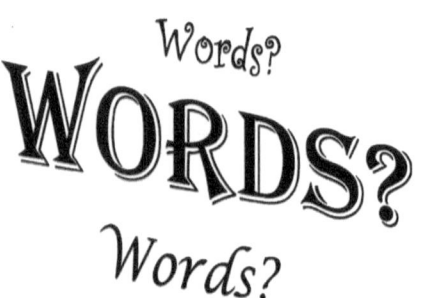

KEY #3
Which Words

If you don't know what to ask for, you won't get far, and you will never get what you need. Well, that's not quite true. What will probably happen? You will stumble and bumble around trying to figure it out or someone will take pity on you and help. How do I know? Because I did stumble and bumble. A lot! And people took pity on me and helped. Eventually, I discovered what worked; still, having *Land Media Interviews Without a Publicist* in my hands would have been a tremendous benefit.

As I began my new adventure, everyone I spoke

with assisted me in my quest to be on radio. After talking to many different people in various positions, I gradually figured out how to ask for the right thing—an interview—and how to get the right answer—yes to an interview. A major component involved learning what receptionists, announcers, producers, etc. were actually talking about. Every industry has its own lingo, and radio is no different. The third key introduces you to the most important terminology and definitions relating to author interviews. Let's get started:

- Announcer: In charge of reading announcements on the air, i.e., the sports announcer, news anchor, or weather reporter. For a small station, the announcer may be the one conducting the interview.
- Broadcast journalism: A catchall term encompassing every aspect of journalism on television and radio, including online news.
- Call letters: Form the ID or official title of a radio station. The ones west of the Mississippi River start with "K" while east of the Mississippi begin with "W." Military stations begin

with "N" or "A." Those in Mexico start with "X" and Canadian ones start with "C."

- Dead air: Time frame when all is silent. Not a good thing on radio, unless it's planned or part of the programming.
- Delayed broadcast: Pre-recorded broadcast playing at a different time than when the recording originally took place.
- Disc Jockey/DJ: Plays songs, gives information, and keeps "dead air" from occurring. The DJ may also conduct interviews, especially when done live.
- Drive time: Time frame when radio stations have the most listeners—Morning Drive (6–10 am) and Afternoon Drive (2–6 pm).
- FCC: Government agency in charge of all things related to radio signals.
- Format: See the definition for "Program format/formatting" below.
- Market: Number of listeners within a radio station's signal, also referred to as listening base or listening audience. A medium market

refers to a city with over 500,000 people; a major market includes the twenty largest cities in the United States.

- Pre-recorded: Refers to programs recorded at an earlier time for playback in a different time slot.
- Producer: A role encompassing many facets. For purposes here, he lines up talent and guests for various programs, which can include author interviews.
- Program director: Determines what content a station will air, with the goal of attracting and keeping a listening audience. He usually decides which author interviews make the cut, if any at all.
- Program format/formatting: Major factor in determining whether stations do author interviews. Streaming, live shows, or pre-recorded segments all play into the decision.
- Programming: The sum total of what a listener hears on a radio, be it country, classical, reli-

gious, news, talk shows, music, etc.

- Streaming: Involves turning audio into digital so programming is heard over the internet or satellite.

Obviously, radio jargon has more than sixteen words to describe the industry. The ones above will give you a heads up when having conversations with radio personnel and some understanding of how radio works. For more definitions, please refer to the website, https://www.radioconnection.com/glossary. Their team put together a lot of great information to help navigate the radio industry.

For your third assignment, familiarize yourself with these definitions. It won't seem like a foreign language when you hear a program director talk about formatting.

NOTES

KEY# 4
Other Media

Writing a book about media interviews can be rather challenging, considering the myriad of options we have before us. At one point, I attempted to interweave podcasts and TV programs in the chapters about radio. My, my, my! Talk about muddying the waters. Instead of a crystal clear lay out, I ended up with something resembling Yellowstone Park's mud pots. Not what a writer wants to convey to an audience. Hence, the fourth key turned into a separate chapter for them.

Thankfully, podcasts and TV programs don't have the same challenges found in radio programming regarding streaming, which saves countless hours. In addition, the websites listing them usually include a brief description, a huge help in the decision-making process.

In the search for podcasts, Google again takes on the role of "Finders/Keepers." Type in the toolbar a phrase like "cooking podcasts" or "sports podcasts" or "women's podcasts", etc. Depending on the topic, hundreds to thousands to millions of websites will pop up. Don't get bogged down with the number, though. Most of them will say "The Top 15 . . ." or something similar. Scan the titles and select the ones that grab your attention. For instance, one titled "Against the Rules" covers a specific aspect in the sports arena. If I wrote a book on athletics, I would put this on my list for a second look.

During my pursuit, I came across a women's site listing over one hundred; however, most of the titles were in stark contrast to my core beliefs so I ignored it. Another Christian site listed over three hundred podcasts. Thinking I hit the jackpot, I clicked on one and discovered I had to sign up separately to get access—for all three hundred.

Not going to happen!

If you do run into a website requiring a signup, use this work-around: Google the name of the program host, which pulls up the host's website. From there, you can decide to pursue it or drop it. Not the quickest solution, but something to consider.

To determine which TV programs might be open to author interviews, include "TV talk shows" after your subject, i.e. Christian TV talk shows, women's TV talk shows, sports TV talk shows. Or use the phrase "Talk shows for . . ." The results will be akin to the outcomes for podcasts.

When looking at an entire TV network, you need to approach each program separately. For instance, The Food Network carries dozens of cooking shows while God TV airs a variety of Christian programming. Do a search for the title of the shows you think will be a good fit and watch Google come through for you. Once you access the websites, find the producer and requirements regarding possible interviews.

Other potential media interviews include newspapers and periodicals. These can open up avenues for speaking opportunities as well. You may already be familiar with some relating to your message. If not, Google can help.

For magazines or journals, make sure your message fits with their market and purpose. How do you determine that? Check out their websites to view their mission statements; then look at their advertisements. You will know exactly who they want to reach along with the message they want heard. The two questions you need to answer—will my message resonate with their audience and does it complement their purpose? If yes, then keep them on your list.

Pursuing newspaper interviews involves a lot more legwork, simply because of the vast number of them. They include not just the small hometown papers, but state, regional, and national ones. In addition, a number of them cater to specific audiences. To determine which ones will work for you, Google newspapers within a state, i.e., newspapers in Kentucky or newspapers with a specific subject matter. Websites will pop up, and you can search through your options. As a side note, most of the smaller ones will be glad to have some new content, especially if you are a local author or at least a resident of the state.

Before moving on, we cannot ignore the various social media platforms at our fingertips. As authors, we know how invaluable they can be in building our platforms and brands. However, they are fast becoming an opportunity to land interviews. Podcasters put out calls on their Facebook pages for authors interested in interviews. A friend of a friend of a friend has another friend who does them. How do you find these prospects? Be watchful and vigilant as you scroll through your home page. Don't automatically ignore sponsored ads; you may discover a hidden gem. Join author groups. Better yet, start your own author group with the goal of helping each other promote your books. Sometimes we have to think outside the box to unlock doors for our message to be heard.

Another source for interviews comes from membership in professional organizations. For instance, the Nonfiction Authors Association emails a weekly list of media leads for members only. The Advanced Writers and Speakers Association (AWSA), a fellowship of

Christian women communicators, has members who host a variety of options for interviews. Of course, most of these groups require dues, but definitely worth looking into for your particular niche.

When researching the terminology common to other media, I found most of it fell into the technical category. Unless you want to dive into the specifics, you don't have to know much of the verbiage outside the title of your contact person. In podcasting and television, your typical connection will be the producer. However, you may talk directly to the host for those with a smaller podcast outreach or a low-power television signal. In print media, your initial contact will most likely be an editor, although the interviewer may be a reporter.

Again, Key #4 provides the nuts and bolts in finding podcasts, TV programs, periodicals, and newspapers for potential author interviews. Due to the feasibility of them, podcasts are in a boom time right now. They're relatively easy to do from the comfort of your own home. For my interview, the podcaster had been given a copy of my book and, after reading it, reached out to me.

With advanced technology, doing a television interview from home isn't out of the realm of possibility anymore. Facebook, Zoom, and others provide face-to-face opportunities for author interviews. You do have a few extra items to consider, such as dress, makeup, background, and lighting. I did one Facebook interview and, unfortunately, did not complete a lighting check. Consequently, my office looked like a cave while viewers could only see my outline. Another hint—don't sit in a chair that swivels. Definitely a few learning curves.

In print media, most interviews will take place over the phone, unless you live in close proximity. Then a face-to-face works great. Another common type of print interview is for authors to respond to a set of questions sent by the reporter/editor. Using this format, you have time to think through the questions and give thoughtful responses.

Your fourth assignment calls for double duty. First, replicate what you did for Key #1. Then, for each media type, apply the same principles found in Key #2, Website Wrangling. Use the Five W's—who, what, when, where, and why. Review the questions and compile the information on your spreadsheet. You may be a pro by now and whip through those websites like a hummingbird gathering nectar. On the other hand, you may feel like a three-toed sloth climbing down a tree. Either way, add these media formats to your list of potential interviews.

NOTES

KEY #5
The Call

Ready for The Call? Probably not. But don't give in to fear. You've invested too much to back out now. For the fifth key, I'm going to present a variety of scenarios you may experience and offer guidance in how to respond. I'll include examples to help you sound professional and polished. Before you punch in the numbers, though, make sure you have your spreadsheet with all relevant information for each station at your fingertips as well as a pen that works. Review the material at hand, and even look over individual websites again to familiarize yourself with specific info. Keep in mind the goal is to talk to the person in charge of program formatting, usually the program director or producer. Another note to consider: While written for radio, you can tweak any of the dialogs to fit the specific media outlet you are contacting or substitute appropriate verbiage.

The Greeting

The station has a program director position listed on its website:

> *"Hello, I'm [NAME], and I'd like to speak to your program director."*

Notice I did not say the person's name. Why? While we may be in the internet/microwave age, people leave stations for a number of reasons, sometimes rather abruptly. No matter how up-to-date you think your information is, a different person could be in that position by the time you call.

The station does not have a program director position listed on its website:

> *"Hello, I'm [NAME], and I'd like to speak to the person who handles your program formatting."*

Depending on the circumstances, you may hear a couple of different responses:

> *"Let me transfer you to [NAME]."*

Write down the name. If you don't, you will probably forget once you start talking to the individual.

> *"I'm sorry, he's not in. Would you like to leave a voicemail?"*

If you choose to leave a voicemail, say the following:

> *"Hello, my name is [NAME], and I have some questions regarding your program formatting. My number is [phone number]. Again, [repeat message.] Thank you and have a great day. Goodbye.*

With this message I did not ask about author interviews. Program directors are extremely busy and, without hearing you directly, may not have the time or take the time to return your call. By leaving a bit of mystery about why you are calling, they usually take the bait to find out more.

If you don't want to leave a voicemail, say the following:

> *"Do you know when he will be back at the station?"or "Do you know when it's a good time to reach him? Also, Does he have a direct line or extension?"*

Again, the goal is to actually make contact with the one in charge of formatting, a somewhat difficult endeavor at times for a variety of reasons. He could be on the air, doing another pre-recorded interview, or at an off-site location. He may also have unusual office hours, especially if he hosts early morning shows. By asking for a direct line or extension, you bypass the "middleman" and can get directly to the person you need.

Occasionally, you will only be able to leave a message with the receptionist or via email. If it's with the receptionist, say:

> *"I have some questions regarding your program formatting."*

At this juncture, you may be given more information about the formatting or directed to a different person to talk to. For email messages, please see Key #7, Sample

A, for an example.

Once in a while on the first hello, you actually reach the person you need to talk to . . .

The program director or person in charge of interviews.

After he introduces himself, say:

> *"Hello, I'm [NAME], and I'm calling to see if your program formatting allows for author interviews."*

With this response I explained exactly why I called. Remember, program directors juggle many things throughout their day. Getting right to the point will be noticed, as will tiptoeing through the jungle. Don't give them a reason to doubt your professionalism. Stay on track.

Response: No.

    Many reasons exist for a "no" answer. Below include the various ones I have encountered:

- The station may stream programming, and you couldn't determine it from your research.
- The station changed the formatting to streaming

after your research.
- The management team does not conduct author interviews, something you couldn't tell from their website.
- The management team does not accept "cold call" requests for interviews. (These are unsolicited calls, similar to unsolicited manuscripts. Personally, I've only had this happen once out of dozens of phone calls.)
- The programming is all paid airtime.
- The station only focuses on interviews with music artists.
- The station is an affiliate/sister under a corporation, which does not have a place for author interviews in the program lineup.
- The station is under new management since you did your research.

If you do get a "no," please be gracious. Thank the person for taking time to listen to your pitch and wish them a good day.

Response: Yes.

Yes! While you may want to do cartwheels, fly through the air on a trapeze, or let out a roar that rivals a lion, do attempt to keep your composure. Professionalism still counts. You don't want to lose your catch before you reel it in.

The program director will then ask about your book. Remember, he not only wants to keep his listening base, but grow it. While you share your passion, his mind tracks with his audience: *How well do you express yourself? What sound will be heard in a car stuck in traffic? Will your message resonate with his customer base? Will they stay tuned in? Will they tell their friends about hearing you on his station? Where will it fit into the programming?*

What can you do to convince him that his listeners need to hear about your book? Make sure your title creates intrigue. Use your best elevator pitch or hook. Let him know how relevant your topic is to his audience and the takeaway value for them. Throw out a statistic or two. Be positive and enthusiastic. Smile—he will notice through the phone.

After hearing your selling points, he most likely will want more information before committing to an interview. He will also request a media kit, a pdf of a chapter, or a copy of the book. Make notes on your spreadsheet so you don't forget what to send him. Get all of his contact information, including:

- Correct spelling of name
- Direct phone number/extension
- Specific email address with subject line topic
- Correct physical address

Sometimes he may give you a generic email address. If he does, ask what to put in the subject line or how to address the email to make sure he receives it. Otherwise, he may not get it. No email, no interview.

On the other hand, he may give you a firm "yes." The two of you will then discuss potential dates and times. Ask how long the interview will last and if it will be live or pre-recorded. Find out when it will air. While we all want the coveted Morning or Afternoon Drive times, he knows which audience will have the best response to your message. As a side note, this is when your research pays off by suggesting a particular program or time slot that looks like a good fit.

Since his role will be to make sure both of you look/sound good on the air, he will definitely want a media kit, pdf of a chapter, or copy of the book prior to the interview. Again, keep track of all the pertinent information before ending the call.

However, the questions he asked himself while listening to you may lead to a "no." Don't forget, radio interviews translate into free advertising for your book. A program director needs to make sure his investment in you will bring positive returns for him, which means satisfied listeners and advertising dollars. If he doesn't think it will happen after hearing about your book, he won't be willing to take the risk. Swallow your disappointment, thank him for his time, and wish him well.

◆

Response: Yes, but you pay a fee.

While most stations do not charge for interviews,

a few do. The fees can range from a minimal amount of around twenty-five dollars to several hundreds of dollars. Your decision depends on several factors:

- Budget: Can I afford the fee? Can I not afford to pay the fee?
- Marketing: Is this the best use of my marketing dollars? How much will it affect other marketing endeavors?
- Timing: Will paying the fee best serve my target audience now? Note that most publishers prefer interviews take place close to the release of your book, either e-book or print format.
- Outreach: Will paying the fee reach my target audience in the locations I want a big impact?

If you want outside input, discuss the pros and cons with more experienced authors. Read articles about the positive/negative aspects. Reach out on social media and ask questions. Once you decide to pursue a "pay for" interview, the program director/host will need some or all of the material discussed under the "yes" response, and you will need all of his contact information listed in the bullet points under the same response. Personally, I have done a few paid interviews, and I was immensely pleased with the results.

Response: Maybe. Sometimes. Possibly. Depends.

Discouraging words? Not at all. They actually open the door to interviews. Everything I wrote about the "yes" response applies here, amped up 1000 percent. A slight exaggeration? Not much. In this situation, you need to make sure you can sell your book at peak performance to turn the "maybe, sometimes, possibly, depends" into a firm "yes."

While hoping for the "yes," realize the more likely scenario will involve checking out you and your book. Should the program director buy into the message you're selling, he will definitely want more information. Follow the process described under the "yes" response for both of you.

Conversely, he still may say "no." Regardless of

the outcome, stay professional and positive.

Response: No turned into a yes.

In the course of dozens of phone calls, I ran into some "no's" which turned into a "yes." Initially, the program director said "no," yet still asked about my book. Once I shared the message, i.e., hook or elevator pitch, his interest piqued, and he asked for more information. I sent what he requested (refer to items under the "yes" response), and, as a result, generated an interview.

Other times after the "no," we continued the conversation. As we talked, something between us would click, he wanted to see the media kit/sample chapter/book, and I wound up with an interview.

The last possible "no" turning to a "yes" involves public broadcasting stations, commonly known as PBS stations. They have to follow stringent guidelines. Any deviation from them can lead to termination of their FCC license, and no one wants that to happen. Because their purpose is to provide education for the good of the community, they cannot advertise products, including books. The work-around for authors? Promote the message, not the book.

What does it look like in practical terms during the interview? The radio host will have a conversation with you, talk about your book, and ask questions.

What can he not do? He cannot tell his audience where to buy the book, encourage them to buy the book, or say the price of the book.

What can he do? He can, and will, refer his audience to your website to find out more about you and your book. While it's not the best scenario, it still allows listeners to hear your heart and your message, which is why you wrote the book in the first place.

To snag an interview on these stations, you need to be somewhat aggressive because PBS program directors will be insistent on "no." Tell them you understand their restrictions and are ok with simply talking about your book because you believe the message will meet a need for his listening audience. Be willing to sacrifice for the greater good— having a positive, even life-changing, impact on people you may never meet face-to-face. It's worth it.

For your fifth assignment, get together with another author, friend, or family member and role-play the various scenarios I described. If you're uncomfortable, keep at it. You may want to record yourself to hear how you sound or to improve your delivery. Feel free to change the verbiage to fit your style. Practice each of them several times so you're prepared when you make the first call. No matter what unfolds after "Hello," maintain a professional standard. And, above all, be gracious, be thankful, be kind.

NOTES

KEY #6
Media Kits

Sounds rather intriguing. Go ahead and send me your media kit.

So said the program director once he heard my pitch. Unfortunately, I didn't have a media kit. I didn't know what was in a media kit. I didn't even know authors needed media kits. Yet, he wanted one. From me.

Which brings us to the sixth key—developing your own media or press kit. After a number of requests for the missing kit, I decided to do my homework. Of course, it involved Google. Different articles explained the purpose for and the process of developing one. After sifting through several, I created mine. Once it was ready, I emailed it to the various radio stations. The positive feedback from program directors led to a number of confirmed interviews. The list below discusses the typical items found in author media/press kits:

Author Bio

You can include up to four different types of bios:
- Two-line—approximately 140 characters, similar to Twitter. Make it power punching.
- Short—approximately 50 words. Focus on a unique aspect of your expertise.
- Medium—approximately 100 words. Include the short bio plus a highlight or accomplishment of your writing profession to help you stand out.
- Long—approximately 400–600 words. Write an overview of your life and writing career.

The interviewer or host will appreciate having several to work with. Although some asked about my preference, I always left it up to each of them to decide.

If you've never written your author bio, begin working on it. The internet has hundreds of articles with suggestions, bullet points, and examples. Browse the bios of your favorite authors. If you find yourself at a loss or get stuck, feel free to contact me, and I will send you some guidelines.

Business/Personal Vision

Successful businesses and individuals have vision statements. Writing down your dreams and/or visions provides a solid foundation for your journey, a vitally important step most authors don't think about. Once you put them on paper, they give direction and purpose, both personally and professionally. Program directors like to see the passion behind the writing. Yes, as authors, our passion is our writing. But why? What do you want to accomplish that is bigger than you? A vision statement encapsulates what's in your heart and lets others hear its beat.

Book Cover

Impressive book covers sell, especially if your book hasn't been released yet. Including it in your media kit will be one more opportunity to hook the interview.

About Page or Sell Sheet or One Sheet

Flipping through magazines, we quickly turn past full-page ads to get to the article we want to read. Occasionally, we pause to check out the product. Why? What stops us from moving on? A beautiful, eye-catching advertisement. This, in essence, is what sell sheets do—promote your book on one piece of paper. Most include:

- Title/Author
- Synopsis (include up to four, similar to the author bios)
- Cover Artist and contact info
- Release Date/Availability
- Formats, i.e., paperback, e-book, etc.
- Book Specifications (Specs), including the ISBN#
- Agent Name and contact info, if represented by a literary agency

You may want to add other information as well. Feel free to Google one sheets or sell sheets for more material and examples.

Book Excerpt

Not only does an excerpt provide a glimpse into your book, it presents a compelling reason to offer an interview. Choose a section to tantalize the program director, who can then entice his listening audience. Or use the back cover copy. It can provide another excellent opportunity to present your book to potential customers.

Photos

Include several of your best photos. Have an assortment of poses and settings, ranging from casual to professional. The variety gives the appearance of someone a listening audience can connect with, which is what a program host looks for.

Press Release

Usually your publisher provides the press release. If you self-publish, you will likely need to do your own.

Again, check the internet for samples. Then adapt your own work and style. Be creative. Come up with a unique angle. Ask a few other people to review it to catch any typos, grammatical errors, etc.

Contact Info

Have all your contact information available here. Include the following:

- Email
- Website
- Social Media links related to your writing
- Phone
- Address
- Agent Name and contact info, if represented by literary agency

Keep it simple. Use bullet points. Make it stress-free for program directors to reach you. If they decide it's too complicated, they won't bother.

Endorsements

Adding endorsements shows radio hosts positive feedback from others who have read your book. It also gives them insight into making the connection between you and their listening base. If readers have left reviews for you on an online bookseller, i.e., Amazon, Barnes and Noble, etc., copy them here.

Interview Questions

Your program host will appreciate this page more than you know. His job is all about sound. How you sound, how he sounds, what sound gets amplified, and what sound his listeners hear. With an opportunity to look over the questions, he can sound knowledgeable, even if he hasn't read your book, and you will sound professional, even if it's your first interview.

Below are ten questions from my media kit for *Making Crooked Places Straight*. While some of them are specific to my book, they will give you a starting place:

- Why did you choose this topic for your first book?
- How long did it take you to write it?
- Each chapter starts with a conversation. Who

is this person and what is his/her role in your book?

- You have some unusual chapter titles. How did you come up with them?
- Why is chapter two so long?
- What were some surprises for you along the journey?
- What is the take away for people when they finish reading *Making Crooked Places Straight*?
- What were some of your challenges in writing *Making Crooked Places Straight*?
- How did your book impact you?
- How can readers connect with you?

As you can see, some fall in the generic category while others directly relate to my book. However, my full list includes questions of a more personal nature. Why add them? They make you real to people hearing your voice while driving home from work, doing laundry, or exercising at the gym. They open you up to a potential fan base and go a long way toward outreach and making connections.

For an added bonus, Appendix A contains my entire list of nearly fifty questions. Feel free to adapt them or piggyback off them to fit you and your book. If personal questions make you too uncomfortable, tailor them to fit your style. Or browse articles on the internet for more possibilities.

Be sure to practice answering the questions. If it helps, write out your responses. You want to feel comfortable and show your expertise at the same time.

Speaking Info

If you combine your writing profession with a speaking career, this page needs to be part of the kit. It allows the radio host to present you as an author and a speaker, which can open doors to numerous opportunities.

You will want to have a title and short synopsis for each topic, no more than one hundred words. It should read like a pitch for your book—enticing and power punching. If you need some examples, Google one sheets for speakers. You can also check out the Speaking page on my website, PS2710.com. For another option, you can add a separate one sheet designed for your topics. Similar to those for books, this type sells you as a speaker.

Logo

Include your logo and any other media-ready work you have available. Many times, stations will advertise upcoming interviews on their social media pages and will include your logo, photo, etc.

No doubt you know what your sixth assignment entails. Yes, putting together your own media kit. Overwhelming? Obviously. Frankly, I was overwhelmed when I began mine. Still, not doing one is not an option.

Start with one section at a time. Parts of it won't take long because you probably have some information stored in another document, and it's a matter of copy and paste. Be encouraged. The piecemeal portions eventually lead to a completed work. If you find yourself stuck, check out mine. The link is on my Speaker page at PS2710.com.

Another important ingredient is creativity. Don't let yours become a run-of-the-mill kit. You are advertising you and your book within these pages. You want program directors to remember you. Let your passion shine.

Once you finish, edit it. Then have two or three people review it. Ask them to check for any errors you might have missed. Then edit it again. Trust me. You'll be glad you did.

NOTES

KEY #7
Follow Up

After the phone call, what's next? Follow-up! The seventh key is critical to landing an interview. Here, we will look at two forms, emails and phone calls. Both play important roles in your quest to be on the air.

The first set of follow-up emails covers those you send after the initial contact with the program director or staff. Before you dispatch them, review your notes. Make sure your attachments are ready to send out, i.e., media kit, sample chapter, etc. I know I discussed this in Key #5, The Call, but don't forget to put down all the information on your spreadsheet or whatever form you choose to use. Include names/dates/attachments, along with any other pertinent material. You will never be able to keep track of it unless you have a system in place. In my pursuit to be on the air, the spreadsheet turned out to be my most valuable tool.

The wording of your email depends on whether you received a definite "yes" response or the "maybe" response. Below are samples of what I sent. The first sentence or two may vary a bit; however, the basic format and information remain the same:

Sample A. Email to program host you have not spoken with for possible interview.

Hi, [NAME]

I'm writing regarding a potential interview with my book *Making Crooked Places Straight*. It's a spiritual warfare training manual, teaching people to recognize how a perverse spirit works in their lives and how to walk in victory over it. I believe it is a timely word for the days we live in, and I think it would benefit your listeners.

I'm attaching a media kit for your review. Please don't hesitate to contact me if you have any questions or need anything else. I look forward to hearing from you.

Sincerely,

Penelope Kaye

As stated above, send an email of this sort to a director you have not spoken to at all. While not a common occurrence, it does happen. A few people in charge of program formatting only respond to emails.

Notice in the first sentence I tell him the purpose of the email, a potential interview for my book, with the title. Next, I add the hook or pitch to grab his attention again. Then I tell him why his listening base will benefit from the interview. Finally, I mention the attachment, offer my services, and include an invitation to contact me.

Sample B. Email to program host you spoke to for possible interview.

Hi, [NAME]

I enjoyed chatting with you about a potential interview for my book *Making Crooked Places Straight*. It's a spiritual warfare training manual, teaching people to recognize how a perverse spirit works in their lives and how to walk in victory over it. I believe it is a timely word for the days we live in, and I think your listeners will benefit from hearing about it.

I'm attaching a media kit for your review. Please don't hesitate to contact me if you have any questions or need anything else. I look forward to hearing from you.

Sincerely,

Penelope Kaye

This email includes all the verbiage in Sample A *and* a reference to the actual phone conversation with him. The reminder of the call will jog his memory in the midst of a hectic day at the station.

◆

Sample C. Email to program host who said yes to an interview.

Hi, [NAME]

I spoke to you about a potential author interview for my book *Making Crooked Places Straight*. It's a spiritual warfare training manual, teaching people to recognize how a perverse spirit works in their lives and how to walk in victory over it. I believe it is a timely word for the days we live in, and I think your listeners will benefit from hearing about it.

You graciously offered to do an interview with me. I'm attaching a media kit for your review. Please don't hesitate to contact me if you have any questions or need anything else. I look forward to hearing from you.

Sincerely,

Penelope Kaye

With the "yes" response, you want to include a reminder of the phone call and his commitment to the interview. Even a definitive "yes" still needs a confirmation in your follow-up.

◆

Sample D. Email to generic inbox or general staff for possible interview.

Hello, [CALL LETTERS] Staff

I'm writing regarding a potential author interview for my book *Making Crooked Places Straight*. It's a spiritual warfare training manual, teaching people to recognize how a perverse spirit works in their lives and how to walk in victory over it. (I spoke with [NAME] regarding it, and he/she requested more information.) I believe it is a timely word for the days we live in, and I think it would be a great benefit to your listeners.

I'm attaching a media kit for your review. Please don't hesitate to contact me if you have any questions or need anything else. I look forward to hearing from you.

Sincerely,

Penelope Kaye

Occasionally, the director or staff member asks you to send the email to the station, not an individual. When that happens, make sure you get the correct call letters for the station and in the correct order.

Only add the information in parentheses as a point of reference if you know the email is not going to the person who gave you the generic address.

For the second type of follow-up, we could pine for

a perfect world where program directors who received our emails would respond promptly in our favor. Uh, yeah, no. Unfortunately, life hits them the same ways it slams into us. They get busy with other things, distracted by other things, or sidelined by other things. Not to mention accidents, crises, or tragedies.

Consequently, we may need to send a second follow-up email or make a follow-up call. Either way can be uncomfortable, albeit understandable. When I found myself in this situation, I always maintained a kind, gracious demeanor, which always resulted in a humble and apologizing radio host. Below are examples of an email and phone call:

Sample E. Email follow-up to program host who has not responded to your original email after the phone call. (Refer to samples B, C, or D.)

> Hi, [NAME]
>
> I'm following up on an email I sent you on [DATE] regarding a potential interview. I chatted with you a while back regarding my book *Making Crooked Places Straight*. It's a spiritual warfare training manual, teaching people to recognize how a perverse spirit

works in their lives and how to walk in victory over it. I believe it is a timely word for the days we live in, and I think it would benefit your listeners.

My media kit is attached for your review. Please don't hesitate to contact me if you have any questions or need anything else. I look forward to hearing from you.

Sincerely,

Penelope Kaye

Here, let him know in the first two sentences that you are sending a follow-up to your original email *because* of the phone call for a potential interview. Since we all know emails get lost in the multitude, are accidentally deleted, disappear into cyber space, land in the spam folder, or never find their home, attach the media kit again. You can also use this format for Sample A; however, leave out the section referencing a phone call.

Sample F. Phone call for follow-up to program host who has not responded to the original email after the phone call. (Refer to samples B, C, or D.)

Hi, [NAME]

> This is Penelope Kaye. I'm doing a follow-up call regarding the email I sent you about a potential author interview for my book Making Crooked Places Straight. I wanted to touch base to see if you received my email with the media kit or if there's anything else you need from me.

If you do reach the person on the phone, he will apologize, and you will reply with "no worries" or something similar. Then move forward with a discussion about your book and the potential interview. If you have to leave a message, you can say the same thing and include your phone number and a good time to reach you.

◆

Send the third kind of follow-up email when you've been in discussions with the program host, and . . . silence. You begin to wonder, *Do I or don't I have an interview?* Again, it can be awkward; yet, as long as you handle it with grace and dignity, you can expect an apologetic response, and potentially a positive outcome. Look at the sample below:

Sample G. Email to program director who has stopped

a back-and-forth discussion for the interview.

> Hi, [NAME]
>
> I'm following up regarding our on-going discussion of a potential author interview for my book Making Crooked Places Straight. It's a spiritual warfare training manual, teaching people to recognize how a perverse spirit works in their lives and how to walk in victory over it. I believe this is a timely word for the days we live in, and I think it would benefit your listeners. My media kit is attached for your review. Please don't hesitate to contact me if you have any questions or need anything else. I look forward to hearing from you.
>
> Sincerely,
>
> Penelope Kaye

In the first sentence, include a reminder of the discussion in progress. The sample above contains the standard wording, although you may want to change it up a bit here. Give the program director two weeks, three at the most, of no contact before sending it out. Remember, life happens. You should receive a reply, and then be able to continue with the dialog.

With these different examples for follow-up, you can move confidently in pursuing radio interviews. In the perfect world I mentioned earlier, each one would result in a resounding "Yes! We want you on our program." However, we don't live in a flawless society. What am I trying to say? Be ready to handle a "No." Because it will come. However, don't give up. Keep calling. Keep sending emails. Keep your focus on what's important: Getting your message heard.

For your seventh assignment, work on the wording of your own follow-up emails. Put them in template forms to copy and paste. Just make sure you change the name and any other info to match the recipient. I forgot to do that once. Yikes! Thankfully, the person who received the misnamed email was very understanding.

One other critical piece in composing emails—*ask what to put in the subject line.* Emails swamp the inbox of most program directors. To make sure yours doesn't end up in a cyberspace trashcan, put a reference to an interview and the title of your book. For instance, *potential author interview/title of book*.

Again, your goal is to generate a radio interview. Make it easy for them to say Yes!

NOTES

KEY #8
The Interview

Having gained valuable insight and instruction through seven keys, we now come to the eighth, and final, one—the actual interview. While you may panic a bit, remember, the program host has probably been conducting interviews for quite a while. He knows how to present a good image for you and his station.

However, you can take steps to alleviate stress and anxiety. By now, any and all calendars you use should have the date and time set. A couple of days before your big event, reach out to your contact person via email or phone to confirm the interview is taking place. As obvious as it might sound, it is a necessary step. Ask if it's your responsibility to call in. If yes, verify the phone number. Discuss any protocols the station follows. Make sure you both know how you each want to be addressed.

The day before, review the questions you sent for the interview. If it helps, write down your answers. Role-play with a friend. Throughout the practice session, get comfortable in your own skin. See yourself engaged in a dialog with another person regarding your book. Because that is exactly what your program host wants—a relaxed conversation about something important to you and his listening base. Even if he wants to discuss a particular topic or theme from your book, he will still approach the interview as an informal chat between the two of you.

For live interviews, you really need to be on your top game. If you do make a mistake, try to cover it as quickly as possible. Since you know your book better than anyone else, pull in a few facts or a favorite quote to move things back in the right direction.

However, most are recorded for later playback. In these instances, the tech people will take care of most issues. Once I forgot to mention my website, so the sound tech added it later. Another time I was caught off guard by an added question after my answer to one from my list. I really scrambled to make my response sound casual and knowledgeable.

A few other hints to help during the interview:
- Do actually answer the questions—easy to dance around the topic, harder to stay focused
- Do give short answers to the questions—easy to get long-winded, harder to condense responses
- Do share appealing stories—easy to sound boring, harder to stay engaged
- Don't talk more than the interviewer—easy to do, harder to control

Fledgling authors tend to forget or may not be aware of these tips. Remember, you are a guest on someone else's program. While the interviewer wants to promote you and your book, you need to show honor and respect to him.

Regarding timing, most interviews run five to ten minutes, although some can last up to an hour. I prefer the longer ones because I have time to relax and find my groove. In one case, the program host left two hours open for the interview. Another time, the plan was for thirty minutes, but once she received my book and media kit with the questions, she extended it to a full hour. Regardless of how much time you have to share your heart for your book, remember the following points:

- Relax: Those drivers in traffic will notice if you come across tense or nervous. Relax.
- Enjoy: Smile. Laugh. Act like you're having fun. If the commute home turns into a traffic jam, they will appreciate it.
- Serve: Remember, you wrote your book for a purpose—to meet a need. Reaching out to the stay-at-home mom, busy executive, over-the-road trucker, or next-door neighbor will be rewarding in itself.

After you've done one or two, these traits will be more natural, and you will develop your own flow when you share your favorite topic.

If possible, take time to chat with your host once you've completed the interview. First, ask for feedback on how he thinks it went. Next, if it was pre-recorded, ask when the station will air it so you can let your fans/following know. Request a copy of the interview to put on your website. Then, follow-up with a thank you note. And always, always be gracious, be thankful, be kind.

Another note, before we close out the last key. I spoke to dozens of program directors and gained valuable information each time. One, whom I now consider a dear friend, responded with profound kindness in my "didn't know diddly-squat" stage. Even more, he gave me insight into behind the scenes of radio, including two golden nuggets of wisdom.

The first one surprised me. He emphatically stated that it is not the responsibility of the author to mention the book title. He said, "Always, always let the program host introduce your book and mention the title. You can refer to a chapter title, but never the book. It's the sign of a novice. Don't do it."

Second, and more importantly, he said, "Just remember, Penelope. When you're on the air, you don't know who's listening. It could be anyone from anywhere around the world. But the real key in radio is to concentrate on the one. Even though you want to have hundreds or thousands listening, keep your focus on the one—the one driver, the one mother, the one businessman—and talk as if *that* person is the only one who hears you."

While his insight is specific to radio, the same principle holds true for other outlets. Why? When it's all said and done, you have entered a realm that is up close and personal. An intimacy develops between the two of you because nothing gets in the way of the sound of your voice to his or her heart. In those moments of traffic jams or housework or sleepless nights, your message resonates across an invisible realm and changes lives.

And that is the most important reason for you, the author of an amazing one-of-a kind book, to pursue media interviews.

Your eighth, and last assignment, will probably be obvious. Similar to the one for Key #5, The Call, practice interviewing. Grab a friend, a cup of coffee or tea, and chat about your book using questions from the list you developed. Get comfortable with your responses. Write down your answers. Record yourself. Practice some more. Then make the call!

NOTES

Author's Note

I sincerely hope you found these eight keys beneficial in your quest for author interviews. Still, the success of obtaining them depends wholly on you. Since you purchased *Land Media Interviews Without a Publicist*, you clearly have the desire to open the door to exciting adventures. Besides, you're an author. You have a gift to share. The world is waiting.

Go ahead. Make the call!

Acknowledgments

Wow! Amazing how an idea becomes a reality, which is how *Land Media Interviews Without a Publicist* came to be. But not without the support from some remarkable people:

> Michael. This absolutely would not have happened without you.
>
> Janet. My test pilot.
>
> Jerry. You know.
>
> Tammy. My rescuer.
>
> Patricia. Brilliant.
>
> Linaya and Wanda. Editors par excellence. (Please use the French pronunciation here.)
>
> My intercessors. Yes!
>
> Oregon Christian Writers and Colorado Write His Answer Conferences. I would never see my name on book covers without them—organizers, editors, agents, authors, and all attendees. You are amazing!

Appendix A

List of Interview Questions

As you can see, I divided the questions into three sections. It gives program directors the opportunity to have you back for more than one interview to cover different aspects of your book. The set titled "Other FAQs" can be used for fun or to avoid dead air if needed.

1. Why did you choose this topic for your first book?
2. How long did it take you to write it?
3. Each chapter starts with a conversation. Who is this person and what is his/her role in your book?
4. You have some unusual chapter titles. How did you come up with them?
5. Why is chapter two so long?
6. What were some surprises for you along the journey?
7. What is the take away for people when they fin-

ish reading *Making Crooked Places Straight*?
8. What were some of your challenges in writing *Making Crooked Places Straight*?
9. How did your book impact you?
10. How can readers connect with you?

1. Book covers are an invitation to readers. Tell us about the creative process involved in making the cover.
2. What is the significance of the title?
3. Who or what was the inspiration for this book?
4. You included a lot of prayers. Why was that?
5. Was there any part of the book you enjoyed writing, other than "The End?"
6. You wrote a chapter about weapons. Why was that important? Do you have a favorite weapon?
7. How does the perverse spirit get access in a person's life, leading to bondage?
8. What was your actual process in writing *Making Crooked Places Straight*?
9. Will there be a sequel?

10. The publishing process can be long and difficult. How did you connect with Morgan James Publishing?

---

1. What were your goals for this book, and how well do you feel you achieved them?
2. What vocabulary words or concepts may be new to readers? Define some of them.
3. What do people THINK they know about your subject/genre, but in reality, they don't?
4. What is the most important thing people DON'T know about your subject/genre that they need to know?
5. You included some illustrations within the chapters. Tell us about them.
6. How did you deal with the emotional impact of this book as you were writing?
7. You wrote about Noah Webster a lot. Why was he so important in your book?
8. What makes your book stand out from the crowd?

9. You included a lot of scripture references in your book. Why was that important?
10. What's your next project?

Feel free to include in all interviews:
- Where can readers purchase your books?
- Where can readers find out more about you and your books?
- Are you available for speaking?

Other FAQs
1. How do you come up with titles for your books?
2. When did you first consider yourself a writer?
3. Who is your favorite author and why?
4. What books or authors have influenced your own writing?
5. Who is the author you most admire in your genre?
6. How many bookshelves are in your house?
7. What do you like to do when you are not writing?
8. What did you want to be when you grew up?
9. What's for dinner tonight? What would you

rather be eating?

10. What's the best part of your day?
11. Share something your readers wouldn't know about you.
12. If you could only have one season, what would it be?
13. If you could cure a disease, what would it be?
14. If you were a tour guide, what would you like a visitor to see and what impression would you want them to take away with them when they leave?
15. What's your favorite spot to visit in your own country? And what makes it so special to you?
16. What are some day jobs you've held? If any of them impacted your writing, share an example.
17. What do you like to read in your free time?

Appendix B

Download Code for Spreadsheet

The spreadsheet template is just that—a template. Feel free to change it to fit your own style and needs. To access it, go to my website, PS2710.com. Once there, look in the bottom left corner for "Download Code." Click on it and choose one of the options to receive the spreadsheet. The following code is case sensitive, but doesn't need to be bolded: **8K3ys!4u!**

www.ingramcontent.com/pod-product-compliance
Lightning Source LLC
Chambersburg PA
CBHW022009120526
44592CB00034B/749